the
2009 STAMP
YEARBOOK

2009 STAMP *the* YEARBOOK

COLLINS REFERENCE
An Imprint of HarperCollins Publishers

UNITED STATES POSTAL SERVICE

HarperCollins books may be purchased for educational, business,
or sales promotional use. For information please write: Special
Markets Department, HarperCollins Publishers, 10 East 53rd Street,
New York, NY 10022.

Designed by Journey Group, Inc.

ISBN 978-0-06-196091-8

09 10 11 12 13 ❖/WZ 10 9 8 7 6 5 4 3 2 1

Complete your *2009 Stamp Yearbook* today! For just $17.50, you'll
get the 33 mail-use stamps featured in the second half of this
book along with the corresponding stamp mounts. To order item
#990904 while supplies last, call 1 800 STAMP-24.

Other books available from the United States Postal Service:
The 2008 Commemorative Stamp Yearbook
The Postal Service Guide to U.S. Stamps — 36th Edition

CONTENTS

| | | | | |

INTRODUCTION

BY :: Dr. Henry Louis Gates, Jr.

Collectible Stamps

EARLY TV MEMORIES

PLACE & DATE OF ISSUE :: North Hollywood, CA, August 11, 2009

ART DIRECTOR & DESIGNER :: Carl T. Herrman

BOB HOPE

PLACE & DATE OF ISSUE :: San Diego, CA, May 29, 2009

ART DIRECTOR & DESIGNER :: Derry Noyes

ARTIST :: Kazuhiko Sano

Legends of Hollywood: GARY COOPER

PLACE & DATE OF ISSUE :: Los Angeles, CA, September 10, 2009

ART DIRECTOR & DESIGNER :: Phil Jordan   ARTIST :: Kazuhiko Sano

CIVIL RIGHTS PIONEERS

PLACE & DATE OF ISSUE :: New York, NY, February 21, 2009

ART DIRECTOR :: Ethel Kessler   DESIGNER :: Greg Berger

JUSTICES OF THE SUPREME COURT OF THE UNITED STATES

PLACE & DATE OF ISSUE :: Washington, DC, September 22, 2009

ART DIRECTOR :: Ethel Kessler

DESIGNER & ILLUSTRATOR :: Lisa Catalone-Castro and Rodolfo Castro

Black Heritage: ANNA JULIA COOPER

PLACE & DATE OF ISSUE :: Washington, DC, June 11, 2009

ART DIRECTOR & DESIGNER :: Ethel Kessler   ARTIST :: Kadir Nelson

ALASKA STATEHOOD

PLACE & DATE OF ISSUE :: Anchorage, AK, January 3, 2009

ART DIRECTOR & DESIGNER :: Phil Jordan   PHOTOGRAPHER :: Jeff Schultz

OREGON STATEHOOD

PLACE & DATE OF ISSUE :: Portland, OR, January 14, 2009

ART DIRECTOR & DESIGNER :: Derry Noyes   ARTIST :: Gregory Manchess

HAWAI'I STATEHOOD

PLACE & DATE OF ISSUE :: Honolulu, HI, August 21, 2009

ART DIRECTOR & DESIGNER :: Phil Jordan   ARTIST :: Herb Kawainui Kane

EDGAR ALLAN POE

PLACE & DATE OF ISSUE :: Richmond, VA, January 16, 2009

ART DIRECTOR & DESIGNER :: Carl T. Herrman   ARTIST :: Michael J. Deas

ABRAHAM LINCOLN

PLACE & DATE OF ISSUE :: Springfield, IL, February 9, 2009

ART DIRECTOR & DESIGNER :: Richard Sheaff   ARTIST :: Mark Summers

GULF COAST LIGHTHOUSES

PLACE & DATE OF ISSUE :: Biloxi, MS, July 23, 2009

ART DIRECTOR & DESIGNER :: Howard E. Paine   ARTIST :: Howard Koslow

THANKSGIVING DAY PARADE

PLACE & DATE OF ISSUE :: New York, NY, September 9, 2009

ART DIRECTOR & DESIGNER :: Howard E. Paine   ARTIST :: Paul Rogers

Nature of America: KELP FOREST

PLACE & DATE OF ISSUE :: Monterey, CA, October 1, 2009

ART DIRECTOR & DESIGNER :: Ethel Kessler   ARTIST :: John D. Dawson

Celebrating Lunar New Year: YEAR OF THE OX

PLACE & DATE OF ISSUE :: New York, NY, January 8, 2009

ART DIRECTOR & DESIGNER :: Ethel Kessler   ARTIST :: Kam Mak

| | | | | |

Mail Use Stamps

Literary Arts: Richard Wright
PLACE & DATE OF ISSUE :: Chicago, IL, April 9, 2009

Polar Bear
PLACE & DATE OF ISSUE :: New York, NY, April 16, 2009

Wedding Rings
PLACE & DATE OF ISSUE :: Washington, DC, May 1, 2009

Wedding Cake
PLACE & DATE OF ISSUE :: Washington, DC, May 1, 2009

U.S. Flag
PLACE & DATE OF ISSUE :: Washington, DC, May 1, 2009,
and May 8, 2009; McLean, VA, June 5, 2009

The Simpsons
PLACE & DATE OF ISSUE :: Los Angeles, CA, May 7, 2009

Love: King & Queen of Hearts
PLACE & DATE OF ISSUE :: Washington, DC, May 8, 2009

Distinguished Americans: Mary Lasker
PLACE & DATE OF ISSUE :: Washington, DC, May 15, 2009

Dolphin
PLACE & DATE OF ISSUE :: Washington, DC, June 12, 2009

Scenic American Landscapes:
Grand Teton National Park, Wyoming
PLACE & DATE OF ISSUE :: Washington, DC, June 28, 2009

Scenic American Landscapes:
Zion National Park, Utah
PLACE & DATE OF ISSUE :: Washington, DC, June 28, 2009

Flags of Our Nation: Set 3
PLACE & DATE OF ISSUE :: Pittsburgh, PA, August 6, 2009

Winter Holidays
PLACE & DATE OF ISSUE :: New York, NY, October 8, 2009

Hanukkah
PLACE & DATE OF ISSUE :: New York, NY, October 8, 2009

Kwanzaa
PLACE & DATE OF ISSUE :: New York, NY, October 9, 2009

Christmas:
Madonna and Sleeping Child by Sassoferrato
PLACE & DATE OF ISSUE :: San Simeon, CA, October 20, 2009

Credits
Acknowledgments

SERVING ON the Citizens' Stamp Advisory Committee is a responsibility that no historian could ever take lightly. The task of representing the breadth of American culture on stamps is humbling, but watching long-planned projects come to fruition brings a satisfaction all its own. This year, I was especially honored to witness the debut of the Civil Rights Pioneers stamps on February 21, when the NAACP met in New York City to celebrate its 100th anniversary.

The Postal Service made history that morning. The stamps received a standing ovation from hundreds of NAACP delegates, and the honorees' family members were there to share in the gratitude and respect. It truly was one of the great days of my life.

The men and women we honor on stamps represent the best of America. They defied conventional wisdom, they showed tremendous character and strength of will, and often they risked their lives for something greater than themselves. Some helped fulfill the promise of America in grand and public ways, while others made progress in private, their lives and labors resonating for decades thereafter.

This year is an inspiring one for stamps. Our pantheon of honorees reminds us that America is a land of poets and entertainers, activists and educators, dedicated public servants and visionary leaders. As stamps take us to Oregon, Alaska, California, Hawai'i, and the shores of the Gulf Coast, we can only marvel at the natural beauty that feeds our ingenuity and nurtures optimism even in difficult times. To explore our country through stamps is to see America as Walt Whitman did: a nation "greater still from what is yet to come."

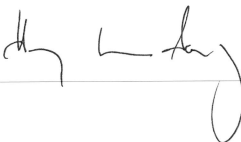

DR. HENRY LOUIS GATES, JR.

Alphonse Fletcher University Professor,
Harvard University

Early TV Memories

IN 1926, the *New York Times* reported the prediction of John Logie Baird, the Scottish inventor of the first working television, that "soon there would be a central broadcasting station where actors would give a show which would be visible on a screen at television theaters some distance away." Two years later, actor Lionel Barrymore suggested to the press that "television will be the next big thing, and we won't have to have any theatres at all." By 1948, one million American homes had television sets—and the predictions of engineers and entertainers alike were starting to prove true.

As the 1950s began, virtually everyone who owned a television watched variety shows, enjoying music and comedy sketches while the hosts, often former nightclub and resort performers, scrambled to understand the impact of the new, intensely visual medium. At the same time, television transformed a familiar American genre, the western, as the success of recycled B movies led the networks to create television westerns for children. The effect on American culture was profound: Instead of hard-bitten, hard-drinking cowboys, these new westerns featured noble, clean-living role models.

ABOUT THE STAMP DESIGNER | Art director Carl T. Herrman worked with twenty2product, a San Francisco–based studio, to give the archival photos on this stamp pane a suitably retro look. The winner of hundreds of design awards, Herrman has directed more than 250 stamp projects, many of them focused on vintage Americana, including Marilyn Monroe, James Dean, Humphrey Bogart, and America on the Move: 50s Fins and Chrome.

PAGE 10

"Television is all the talk— and all the talk is big. . . . Whether the prodigy will live up to its pressagentry, or whether its blessing will be unmixed,

— *Time* magazine, May 24, 1948

As the 1950s progressed, salesmen touted the benefits of television for children. As a result, sales of television sets increased, sometimes to as many as 20,000 a day. By the end of the decade, televisions were in nine out of 10 American homes, and a second wave of Hollywood studios entered the industry. As westerns for adults became popular and dramatic family shows gave way to situation comedies, American television successfully passed from its infancy, ceasing to be an offshoot of either radio or theater to become a powerful medium in its own right.

These stamps commemorate 20 great shows from that golden age, an era when every flicker of the small screen promised the excitement of the new. Decades later, many baby boomers still fondly recall laughing at sitcoms, thrilling to crime dramas, and identifying with ordinary people on game shows—a profound nostalgia nurtured by a young medium intertwined with the collective childhood of a generation.

"Never was an invention so eagerly awaited."

— *New York Times* editorial,
January 27, 1935

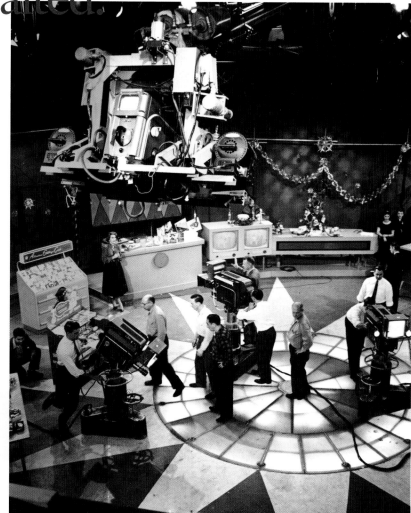

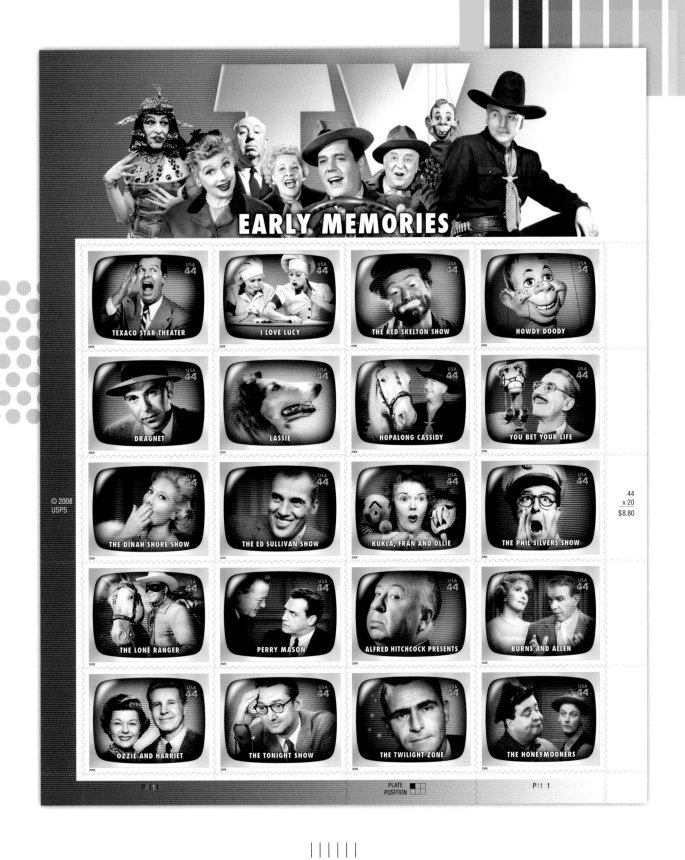

Bob Hope

"THOSE WERE REALLY TOUGH TIMES," Bob Hope quipped about his vaudeville years. "I wouldn't have had anything to eat if it wasn't for the audience throwing stuff at me." A born entertainer, the young singer and dancer first teamed with several partners, but when he found that adding jokes to his act made for happier audiences, he opted to go solo, a decision that made him one of the most beloved entertainers of the 20th century.

During the early 1930s, Hope performed on Broadway, delighting audiences in the musical revue *Ballyhoo* and earning fans as the amiable, wisecracking Huckleberry Haines in *Roberta*. In 1938, after guest appearances on radio shows, Hope headlined his own NBC radio program, opening each highly rated show with a topical monologue of jokes of the kind now commonplace on late-night television.

In his first major film role—Buzz Fielding in *The Big Broadcast of 1938*—Hope impressed audiences and producers alike and crooned "Thanks for the Memory," which would become his theme song. More than 50 films followed, including the famous Road pictures with Bing Crosby, and soon television came calling: In April 1950, Hope headlined an Easter Sunday television special, the first of nearly 300 comedy-variety specials over the years. Hope emceed more Academy Awards presentations than anyone else and was present for numerous milestones, including the first live Oscars telecast in 1953 and the first color broadcast in 1966.

Although Hope never officially served in the U.S. Armed Forces, he was committed to entertaining America's men and women in uniform, starting in 1941 and continuing through Operation Desert Storm five decades later. Hope's many honors included the Congressional Gold Medal and the Presidential Medal of Freedom, but becoming a national treasure couldn't make the wisecracks stop. "I do benefits for all religions," Hope once declared. "I'd hate to blow the hereafter on a technicality."

"I have seen what a laugh can do. It can transform almost unbearable tears into something bearable, even hopeful."

Thanks *for the* Memory

BOB HOPE DEPLOYED so many one-liners during his long career that his 85,000-page joke file is now in the collection of the Library of Congress. Quite a few of those jokes shine with Hope's trademark self-deprecation. To wit:

"I remember my staff asking me when I was going to retire. I said, 'When I can no longer hear the sound of laughter.' They said, 'That never stopped you before.'"

"I consider myself very fortunate. I owe everything to my family and my makeup man. My family kept me going, and my makeup man keeps me from looking like I already went."

"I'm really thrilled tonight, because they requested me to keep appearing before military audiences. The request came from civilian audiences."

PAGE 16

"I would have won the Academy Award if not for one thing: my pictures. Oscar night at my house is called Passover."

Bob and Dolores Hope on a break from a USO performance.

THE LIFE OF HOPE

1903
Leslie Townes Hope born in Eltham, England

1908
The Hope family emigrates to the United States and settles in Cleveland, Ohio

1931-1932
Hope achieves vaudeville success in New York City

1932
Performs in the Broadway musical revue *Ballyhoo*

1936
Performs on stage in the *Ziegfeld Follies* and *Red, Hot, and Blue*

1938
Begins headlining his own NBC radio program and earns a major role in the first of more than 50 feature films

1950
Headlines the first of nearly 300 comedy-variety television specials for NBC

1953
Receives the first of two honorary Academy Awards

1959
Receives the Jean Hersholt Humanitarian Award

1997
Becomes the first person recognized by Congress as "an honorary veteran of the United States Armed Forces"

2003
Dies in California on July 27, two months after his 100th birthday

Gary Cooper

WHETHER GRACING the silver screen as a cowboy, captain, doctor, or soldier, Gary Cooper was the all-American hero. Acclaimed for his believable performances, Cooper was renowned for his strong, silent appeal. He was, in the words of Frank Capra, "a man's man … but a woman's idol"—although amazingly, the icon of 20th-century film almost didn't become an actor at all.

Born in 1901 in Helena, Montana, Frank James Cooper spent his early years on his family's ranch. After attending Grinnell College in Iowa, he considered a career not as an actor but as a political cartoonist, an endeavor that provided little in the way of regular income. While looking for steady work, he ran into friends who

ABOUT THE STAMP ARTIST | Artist Kazuhiko Sano based his portrait of Gary Cooper on a black-and-white photograph taken by George Hurrell around 1940. No stranger to the art of Hollywood, Sano has created advertising illustrations and movie promotions for many prestigious clients during his 30-year career. His work for the U.S. stamp program includes the Celebrate The Century: The 1970s pane.

suggested he become an extra in western films. The job paid $10 a day to fall off a horse; to Cooper this seemed like a great deal of money.

After working as an extra in several films, Cooper was persuaded by a casting agent to adopt the name Gary—after the agent's hometown in Indiana—because Hollywood already had two Frank Coopers. In 1926, when one of the stars of *The Winning of Barbara Worth* backed out at the last minute, Cooper earned a promotion from bit player to lead. Though inexperienced, he gave a convincing performance that was praised by moviegoers and critics. Starring roles soon followed, and Cooper became the rare actor whose career survived and even thrived as silent films gave way to talkies.

Although Cooper excelled in a wide range of genres, he seemed particularly at home in westerns, and his Oscar-winning turn as Marshal Will Kane in the 1952 classic *High Noon* is often considered his finest performance. With characteristic modesty, he once offered a poignant reason for his love of the genre that also explained why fans found him so believable: Westerns reminded him of being back home on the ranch.

Cooper moved audiences as Lou Gehrig in the 1942 classic *The Pride of the Yankees*.

COOPER'S LEGENDS

All told, Gary Cooper appeared in more than 100 movies, including these fan favorites.

1929 — *The Virginian*

1930 — *Morocco*

1932 — *A Farewell to Arms*

1936 — *Mr. Deeds Goes to Town*

1939 — *Beau Geste*

1941 — *Meet John Doe*

1942 — *The Pride of the Yankees*

1943 — *For Whom the Bell Tolls*

1952 — *High Noon*

In the 1954 film *Vera Cruz*, Cooper excelled as a rogue who finds adventure in Mexico.

"The general consensus seems to be that I don't act at all."

Civil Rights
Pioneers

THE MEN AND WOMEN who led the struggle for African-American civil rights were paragons of courage and commitment. With these stamps, the U.S. Postal Service honors the achievements of 12 civil rights leaders, each of whom helped to energize a movement that spanned generations—and to whom future generations owe a profound debt of gratitude.

In 1908, journalist and social worker **Mary White Ovington (1865–1951)** organized a committee to discuss racial issues. Signed by more than 50 prominent citizens, both black and white, their call for a national conference on the problems of black Americans led to the creation of the NAACP, with Ovington serving in various executive positions for nearly 40 years. "So closely is the life of Mary White Ovington woven into the work of the National Association for the Advancement of Colored People," the *New York Times* concluded, "that to talk of one is to talk of the other."

Throughout her life, as a writer,

(continued on page 22)

FROM "THE CALL," ISSUED IN 1909 | "Silence under these conditions means tacit approval. The indifference of the North is already responsible for more than one assault upon democracy, and every such attack reacts as unfavorably upon whites as upon blacks. Discrimination once permitted cannot be bridled; recent history in the South shows that in forging chains for the Negroes the white voters are forging chains for themselves. 'A house divided against itself cannot stand'; this government cannot exist half-slave and half-free any better today than it could in 1861..."

1909
The NAACP is founded

1948
President Harry S. Truman ends segregation in the military

1954
In *Brown v. Board of Education of Topeka,* the U.S. Supreme Court rules school segregation unconstitutional

1955
Rosa Parks arrested for refusing to move to the back of a bus in Montgomery, Alabama; massive boycotts follow; segregation banned on interstate buses and trains

CONTINUED...

"I am sick and tired of being sick and tired."

—*Fannie Lou Hamer*

1957
Nine black students barred from attending Little Rock High School; President Dwight D. Eisenhower uses federal troops to help them enter the school

1960
Four African-American college students begin sit-ins at a Greensboro, North Carolina, restaurant that denies service to black customers

1960
Freedom Riders begin traveling to Southern states

1962
The U.S. Supreme Court rules segregation in transportation facilities unconstitutional; President John F. Kennedy sends federal troops to the University of Mississippi to quell riots over the school's first black student

1963
Dr. Martin Luther King, Jr., delivers his "I Have a Dream" speech in Washington, DC

1964
The Civil Rights Act makes racial discrimination illegal; the 24th amendment abolishes the poll tax

activist, and lecturer, **Mary Church Terrell (1863–1954)** was a powerful advocate for racial justice and women's rights. She worked for decades to win the vote for women and was also one of the prominent citizens who signed "The Call" for the organization of the NAACP. An advocate of protest and resistance against injustice, Terrell endorsed boycotts, sit-ins, and picket lines and remained active into her late 80s.

Many important battles were fought in the courts, and lawyers like **J. R. Clifford (1848–1933)** of West Virginia helped lead the way. In one case, he represented an African-American who wanted his children to attend the local white school since there was no school for blacks. While Clifford did not prevail, the court cited the county's neglect of its black citizens, and a "colored school" was established. In 1898, in a case stemming from a decision to shorten the school year for black children, Clifford won before a jury and on appeal before the state Supreme Court, bolstering arguments for equal rights in education.

The prestigious Spingarn Medal, for "the man or woman of African descent and American citizenship who has made the highest achievement during the preceding year in any honorable field," bears the name of educator, literary critic, and horticulturalist **Joel Elias Spingarn (1875–1939),** who helped develop the NAACP during its early years. Known for his skillful leadership, he countered negative media coverage of African-Americans with an award to highlight black achievement; the first Spingarn Medal was presented to biologist Ernest E. Just.

When reports of racial violence in Illinois in 1908 spurred Mary White Ovington to rally concerned citizens, publishing magnate **Oswald Garrison Villard (1872–1949)** drafted a statement proposing a conference devoted to the complete emancipation of black Americans. Issued on the centennial of Lincoln's birth, "The Call" decrying racial discrimination was signed by a large group of prominent citizens, both black and white, and resulted

DAISY GATSON BATES

1965	1967	1968	1983	1989	2008
Civil rights activists march from Selma to Montgomery, Alabama; passage of the Voting Rights Act	Thurgood Marshall becomes the first African-American on the U.S. Supreme Court	Martin Luther King, Jr., assassinated; President Lyndon B. Johnson signs legislation ending housing discrimination	Federal holiday for Martin Luther King, Jr., established	L. Douglas Wilder of Virginia becomes the first elected African-American governor	Barack Obama elected the first African-American president of the United States

WALTER WHITE · CHARLES HAMILTON HOUSTON

in the formation of the NAACP. With its incorporation in 1911, Villard was named chairman of its board of directors.

In 1957, the enrollment of nine black students at Little Rock's Central High School represented a highly visible challenge to school segregation. Their advisor and central supporter was journalist **Daisy Gatson Bates (1914–1999)**, president of the Arkansas NAACP and advisor to the organization's local Youth Council. Undaunted by death threats, she offered her home as an organizational hub for the Little Rock Nine; in 1958 she joined Martin Luther King, Jr., and others in watching Ernie Green, the only senior among the nine students, receive his diploma.

Many of the lawyers who challenged the faulty legal doctrine of "separate but equal" were trained by one man, **Charles Hamilton Houston (1895–1950).** As chief counsel of the NAACP, Houston formulated a strategy for ending segregation that concentrated first on education, working from the college level down, on the theory that integrating older students would be

"We had to continue the struggle, whatever the cost, to make effective what should have been settled for all time by the Fourteenth and Fifteenth Amendments—the right of every qualified citizen to vote regardless of race."

— Walter White

less threatening to the public. As one of the architects of the civil rights movement, he trained Thurgood Marshall, who succeeded him as chief counsel of the NAACP and later became a U.S. Supreme Court Justice.

With his straight blond hair, blue eyes, and fair complexion, **Walter White (1893–1955)** chose to challenge people's perceptions by identifying as black, but his appearance enabled his undercover investigations of racially motivated violence. White lobbied for civil rights legislation, protested discrimination in the military, and argued against school segregation. Under his leadership, the NAACP became a major force at a time when integration was widely regarded as a radical notion.

The African-American struggle for civil rights claimed many martyrs, including **Medgar Evers (1925–1963).** As the NAACP's first field secretary in Mississippi, Evers led voter registration drives, organized boycotts, and investigated racial violence against African-Americans. Working undercover, he investigated the murder of Emmett Till, a black youth from

MEDGAR
EVERS

Chicago who was killed while visiting relatives in Mississippi. As his achievements were recognized, Evers became more visible to both friends and enemies, and he was murdered at the age of 37. His killer was ultimately convicted; Evers was posthumously awarded the Spingarn Medal.

Fannie Lou Hamer (1917–1977) knew that lack of access to the political process was a key factor in the oppression of black Americans: In 1962, when she tried to register to vote, Hamer lost her job and was beaten and shot at. In 1964, she and an integrated slate of delegates representing the Mississippi Freedom Democratic Party attended the Democratic National Convention and argued that theirs was the legitimate Mississippi delegation since it was the only one open to all citizens of voting age. The "freedom delegates" made an unforgettable impression: Hamer was a delegate to the Democratic National Convention in 1968.

In the 1950s and '60s, as the focus of the civil rights movement shifted from North to South and from courtrooms to direct action, **Ella Baker (1903–1986)** became a vital link between generations. In 1960, after the eruption of the lunch counter sit-in movement, Baker helped students realize they were an important social force in their own right. She organized a conference for student leaders that led to the creation of SNCC, the Student Nonviolent Coordinating Committee.

A courageous and capable woman, **Ruby Hurley (1909–1980)** developed a local NAACP youth council in Washington, DC, and traveled the country during the 1940s dramatically increasing the number of college chapters and youth councils. In Alabama, she faced fierce opposition when she opened the first full-time NAACP office in the Deep South; as she organized new branches and investigated violent racial crimes, she was frequently subjected to death threats and violence.

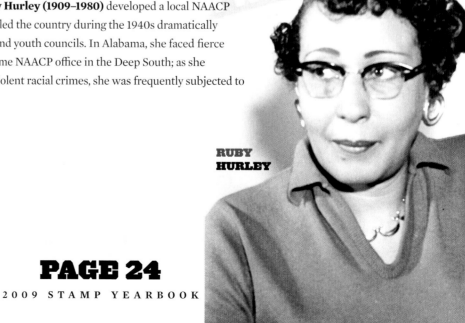

RUBY
HURLEY

"The major job was getting people to understand that they had something within their power that they could use, and it could only be used if they understood what was happening and how group action could counter violence, even when it was perpetrated by the police or, in some instances, the state."

– Ella Baker

ELLA BAKER

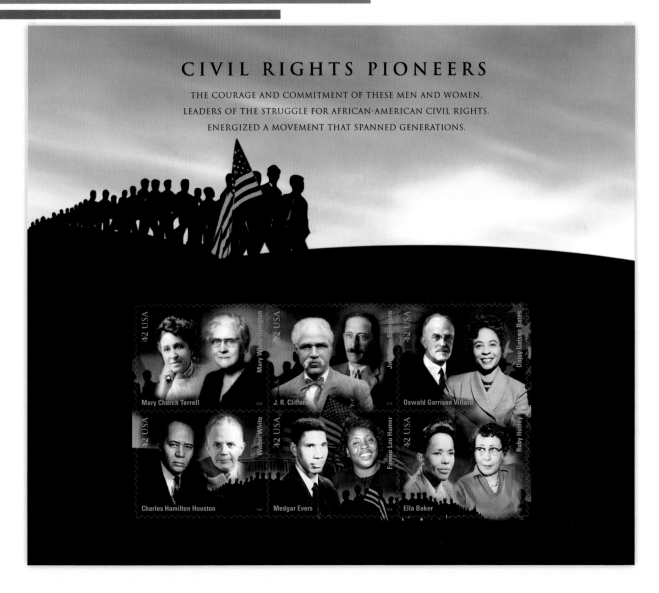

CIVIL RIGHTS PIONEERS

THE COURAGE AND COMMITMENT OF THESE MEN AND WOMEN,
LEADERS OF THE STRUGGLE FOR AFRICAN-AMERICAN CIVIL RIGHTS,
ENERGIZED A MOVEMENT THAT SPANNED GENERATIONS.

Mary Church Terrell

Mary White Ovington

J. R. Clifford

Joel Elias Spingarn

Oswald Garrison Villard

Daisy Gatson Bates

Charles Hamilton Houston

Walter White

Medgar Evers

Fannie Lou Hamer

Ella Baker

Ruby Hurley

Justices
of the Supreme Court
of the United States

"THE SUPREME COURT'S only armor is the cloak of public trust; its sole ammunition, the collective hopes of our society," said Federal Judge Irving R. Kaufman, noting the ability of jurisprudence to change the course of American history. With these four stamps, the U.S. Postal Service commemorates four U.S. Supreme Court justices who contributed to key debates in American life—debates that occur where law and society intersect.

The author of dozens of volumes of legal commentary, **Joseph Story (1779–1845)** gave shape to American jurisprudence while also making the law more accessible to practicing attorneys. His view of law as a science made him one of the nation's most influential jurists, and his devotion to the uniform enforcement of federal regulations by all the states helped establish the preeminence of the Supreme Court.

Louis D. Brandeis (1856–1941) was the associate justice most responsible for helping the Supreme Court shape the tools it needed to interpret the Constitution in light of the sociological and economic conditions of the 20th century. "If we would guide by the light of reason," he once exhorted his colleagues, "we must let our minds be bold." A progressive and a champion of reform, Brandeis devoted his life to social justice. He defended the right of every citizen to speak freely, and his groundbreaking conception of the right to privacy continues to impact legal thought today.

ABOUT THE DESIGNERS
Drawing upon their wide-ranging backgrounds in graphic design, Rodolfo Castro and Lisa Catalone-Castro made sure these stamps featured not only striking portraits of each honoree but also appropriate background elements. Sharp-eyed stamp buyers will notice a photograph of the Supreme Court Building, the official Supreme Court seal, and the first page of the U.S. Constitution. "Our goal," the designers explain, "was to give the historic subject matter a timeless as well as modern feel."

Arguably one of the most enigmatic and controversial figures ever to sit on the Supreme Court, **Felix Frankfurter (1882–1965)** was its strongest proponent of judicial restraint. Frankfurter, who served 23 years as an associate justice, believed that judges should disregard their own social views when making decisions. "History teaches," he wrote, "that the independence of the judiciary is jeopardized when courts become embroiled in the passions of the day."

The author of numerous landmark decisions and the inspiration behind many others, **William J. Brennan, Jr. (1906–1997)** believed that law is an essential force for social and political change. Brennan—the court's most determined opponent of the death penalty—championed equal rights for all citizens and steadfastly regarded the Constitution as a living document that should be interpreted to fit modern life. "The genius of the Constitution," he declared, "rests not in any static meaning in a world that is dead and gone, but in the adaptability of its great principles to cope with current problems and current needs."

JOSEPH STORY USA 44

LOUIS BRANDEIS USA 44

WILLIAM BRENNAN USA

FELIX FRANKFURTER USA 44

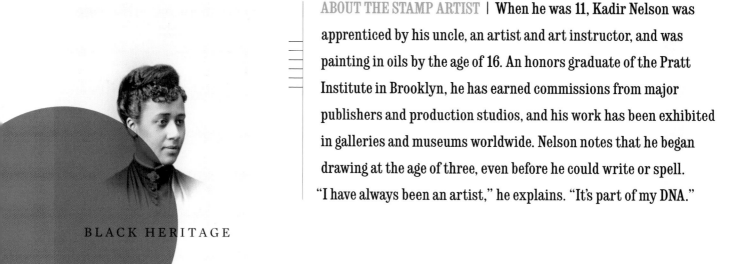

When he was 11, Kadir Nelson was apprenticed by his uncle, an artist and art instructor, and was painting in oils by the age of 16. An honors graduate of the Pratt Institute in Brooklyn, he has earned commissions from major publishers and production studios, and his work has been exhibited in galleries and museums worldwide. Nelson notes that he began drawing at the age of three, even before he could write or spell. "I have always been an artist," he explains. "It's part of my DNA."

BLACK HERITAGE

Anna Julia Cooper

WITH A REMARKABLE LIFE that spanned the end of slavery to the beginning of the civil rights movement, **Anna Julia Cooper (circa 1858–1964)** knew that her calling was "the education of neglected people." Prompted by the idea that education was a means of true liberation, she earned a deserved reputation as a prominent scholar, feminist, and activist.

Born into slavery in North Carolina, Cooper enrolled in Oberlin College in 1881 and became one of the first African-American women to graduate from the school. After teaching mathematics, Greek, and Latin in North Carolina, she was invited to Washington, DC, in 1887 to teach at the Preparatory High School for Colored Youth, the nation's largest and most prestigious public high school for African Americans. When she became principal in 1902, she strengthened the curriculum to prepare students for some of the nation's top colleges and universities. Serving as her own example, she later studied in Paris, becoming the fourth African-American woman to earn a PhD and the first black woman from any country to do so at the Sorbonne.

Because white women routinely excluded them from the growing feminist movement, Cooper and other African-American women created clubs and associations that addressed such issues as education, housing, and unemployment. Despite her prominence, she remained resistant to praise. "I ask no medal in bronze or gold," she wrote in 1925. "There is nothing in life really worth striving for but the esteem of just men that follows a sincere effort to serve to the best of one's powers in the advancement of one's generation."

BLACK HERITAGE

Anna Julia Cooper

USA 44

"My 'racial philosophy' is not far removed from my general philosophy of life: that the greatest happiness comes from altruistic service, and this is in reach of all of whatever race or condition."

Alaska Statehood

IN 1867, when Secretary of State William H. Seward wanted the United States to purchase Alaska from Russia, much of the country was skeptical. Critics in Washington, DC, and more than a few newspaper editorialists derided the notion, calling it "Seward's folly" and "Seward's icebox," and they joked about the establishment of an American polar bear garden in the frozen north.

Fortunately, Seward would not be deterred. Finding an ally in Massachusetts Senator Charles Sumner, chair of the Senate Foreign Relations Committee, Seward continued his campaign. On March 30, 1867, after late-night negotiations in Washington, Russia agreed to sell Alaska for $7.2 million. The transfer to the United States became official on October 18, 1867.

In the years that followed, Seward was vindicated: Several well-publicized gold discoveries boosted interest in Alaska and prompted an increase in the population. Alaska became an official U.S. territory in 1912 and the 49th state on January 3, 1959. Today, much of Alaska consists of parks, forests, and wildlife refuges managed by the federal government, and countless Americans benefit from such vital Alaskan industries as oil and gas, mining, seafood, timber, and tourism—all because one secretary of state saw possibility where others saw only folly.

THE FIRST ALASKANS | In the 49th state, reminders of Native heritage are never far away. The name "Alaska" derives from an Aleut word that means "great land," and approximately 16 percent of the state's population consists of the Tlingit, Athabascan, Aleut, and other Native peoples who migrated to the area some 10,000 years ago. Their story continues to this day: In 1971, the Alaska Native Claims Settlement Act granted Alaskan Natives the rights to approximately 10 percent of Alaskan land and nearly $1 billion in federal compensation and mineral revenues. Distributed by regional and local corporations, these funds insure that Alaskan Natives remain crucial not only to the state's history, but also to its future.

ABOUT THE PHOTOGRAPHER | Since moving to Alaska in 1978, Jeff Schultz has become one of the state's premier photographers, introducing the world to Alaska through his work for books, magazines, and advertisements. Today, Schultz owns and operates Alaska's largest stock photo agency, but he still spends plenty of time out in the field—as shown by this stamp, which features his photograph of a lone dog musher in 2000 near Rainy Pass in the Alaska Range.

Oregon Statehood

WITH THE ISSUANCE of this stamp in 2009, the U.S. Postal Service commemorates the sesquicentennial of Oregon's statehood. Oregon was officially welcomed as the 33rd state on February 14, 1859. Today, Oregon boasts a diverse population, an active and innovative urban scene, and some of the most beautiful and fertile landscapes in the country.

Within a few decades of the Lewis and Clark expedition into Columbia River country, overland immigrants from the East began to pour into the New Eden. By the mid-1800s, thousands had followed the Oregon Trail with dreams of owning land and starting a new life. The Oregon Donation Land Act of 1850 granted as much as 320 acres of land to male settlers and an additional 320 acres to their wives, which spurred some hasty marriages. Of course, American settlers weren't the only inhabitants. Native Americans had been living in the area for countless generations, and Spanish and British groups were making claims as well.

For almost 30 years, the U.S. and Britain jointly occupied the territory, but tension was brewing over borders and natural resources. In 1846, the countries agreed on a boundary at the 49th parallel, now part of the U.S.-Canadian border. The new Oregon Territory included present-day Oregon, Washington, Idaho, and western Montana and Wyoming. The land was split into the Oregon and Washington Territories in 1853. The Oregonians formed a provisional government and agreed on a state constitution. On February 14, 1859, President James Buchanan signed the legislation granting statehood to Oregon.

ABOUT THE STAMP ARTIST

A resident of Beaverton, Oregon, artist Gregory Manchess recalled his own experiences along the Pacific coast to create an evocative painting that incorporates several elements of the coastline — trees, rocks, cliffs, and pounding surf — without illustrating a specific place. "I wanted to make it an icon, an impression, of what the shoreline feels like when you look at the stamp," Manchess says.

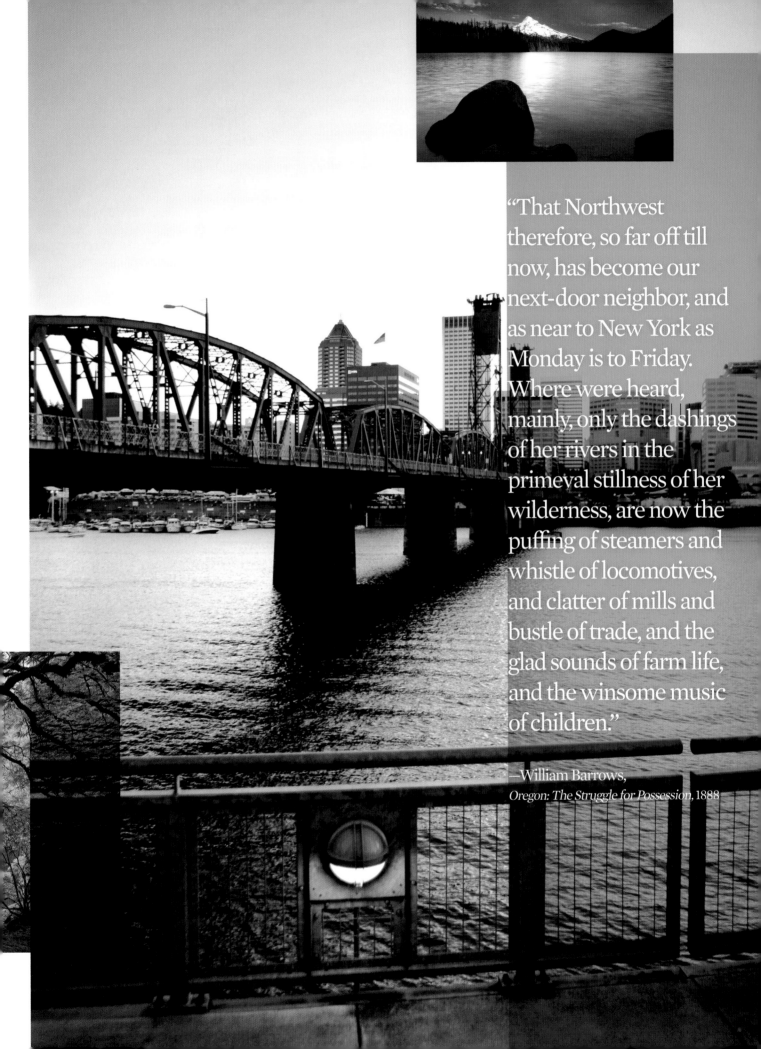

"That Northwest therefore, so far off till now, has become our next-door neighbor, and as near to New York as Monday is to Friday. Where were heard, mainly, only the dashings of her rivers in the primeval stillness of her wilderness, are now the puffing of steamers and whistle of locomotives, and clatter of mills and bustle of trade, and the glad sounds of farm life, and the winsome music of children."

—William Barrows,
Oregon: The Struggle for Possession, 1888

ABOUT THE STAMP ARTIST | Artist and historian Herb Kawainui Kane has dedicated much of his life to studying Hawaiian culture and history. In the stamp art, a surfer rides a wave on a longboard, a popular choice among surfers for centuries. Next to him, two people paddle an outrigger canoe to shore. Kane has extensive knowledge and experience in surfing and in canoe construction, a skill he developed from building a traditional sailing canoe himself.

HAWAI'I
1959   USA 44

Hawai'i Statehood

MADE UP OF EIGHT main islands and more than a hundred smaller ones, the Aloha State owes its existence to volcanic activity and its charm to its enduring beauty. Each year, more than 7 million visitors marvel at the tropical paradise that awaits them, an array of sandy beaches, fertile valleys, and stunning volcanic mountains praised by Mark Twain as "the loveliest fleet of islands that lies anchored in any ocean."

Visitors to Hawai'i are also charmed by the 1.2 million residents whose interwoven cultures are as diverse as the state's geography. With no ethnic majority, the population includes Native Hawaiians, Caucasians, Japanese, other Pacific Islanders, Filipinos, Chinese, Vietnamese, Koreans, and numerous others. The state is also bilingual; after a steep decline in the use of the Hawaiian language in the early 1900s, Hawaiians began reviving their language and culture in the 1970s.

What unites Hawaiians is a set of common values: shared cultural traditions, a reverence for their land and ancestors, and deep respect for their extended family, or 'ohana. Many visitors will praise either Hawaiian culture or the incredible beauty of the 50th state, but Hawaiians know that the land and the people are inseparable; together, they create a special place that Paul Theroux called "not a state of mind, but a state of grace."

circa 500
Polynesians settle the islands

circa 900–1000
Tahitians bring their culture to Hawaiian shores

1778
Captain James Cook arrives from England and names the islands after the Earl of Sandwich

1810
King Kamehameha I unites the islands under a monarchical government

1893
A small group of mostly non-Hawaiian citizens and foreigners overthrows Queen Lili'uokalani

1898
Hawai'i becomes a U.S. territory

1941
The Japanese attack on Pearl Harbor brings thousands of Americans to the island during World War II

1959
Hawai'i becomes the 50th state

Edgar Allan Poe

"POE WAS BORN a poet, his mind is stamped with the impress of genius," one literary critic declared in 1843. "He is, perhaps, the most original writer that ever existed in America." This year, the U.S. Postal Service commemorates the 200th anniversary of the birth of a writer whose appeal has endured for more than a century and a half, and whose troubled life is inseparable from his extraordinary body of work.

Edgar Poe was born in Boston in 1809 and lost both of his parents, actors David Poe and Elizabeth Arnold Poe, before his

(continued on page 38)

FROM "THE RAVEN"

And the Raven, never flitting, still is sitting, *still* is sitting

On the pallid bust of Pallas just above my chamber door;

And his eyes have all the seeming of a demon's that is dreaming,

And the lamp-light o'er him streaming throws his shadow on the floor;

And my soul from out that shadow that lies floating on the floor

Shall be lifted—nevermore!

PAGE 36

ABOUT THE ARTIST

The portrait of Poe on this stamp is an oil painting by award-winning artist Michael J. Deas, whose research over the years has made him well acquainted with Poe's appearance. In 1989, Deas published *The Portraits and Daguerreotypes of Edgar Allan Poe*, a comprehensive collection of images featuring authentic likenesses as well as derivative portraits. Deas has been awarded five medals by the Society of Illustrators, including gold medals for stamp artwork honoring James Dean and Thornton Wilder.

third birthday. Many years later, he would share his feelings about the early loss of his parents in a letter to a man who had known his mother: "I have many occasional dealings with Adversity," he wrote, "but the want of parental affection has been the heaviest of my trials." Poe grew up in the care of John and Frances Allan, wealthy residents of Richmond, Virginia. Although the Allans shared their name with Poe, they never formally adopted him.

Poe enrolled at the University of Virginia in 1826 but withdrew after only one term because of financial difficulties. For the next several years, he struggled to get by and to get his writing into print, surviving with help from his relatives in Baltimore and by joining the U.S. Army. His fortunes took a turn for the better in October 1833, when he won a short-story contest sponsored by a Baltimore newspaper, earning $50 in prize money and greatly improving his job prospects. Two years later, he accepted a job as editor for the *Southern Literary Messenger* in Richmond,

where he published many of his own works and added "literary critic" to his résumé.

From 1838 to 1844, Poe, his devoted wife, and his supportive mother-in-law resided in Philadelphia, where he took an editorial position at a magazine and published some of his most terrifying tales, including "The Tell-Tale Heart," "The Pit and the Pendulum," and "The Gold-Bug." That same year, he also published his book *Prose Romances* and began a popular lecture series on poetry, which he defined as "the rhythmical creation of beauty." Poe's own verse was rich in allusion and atmosphere, with a rhythmical style suggestive of song, hence the memorable meter of "The Raven," which he

published in 1845, one year after moving to New York City. The poem made Poe a star of literary society—yet his income, which continued to come mostly from work at periodicals, was never more than barely adequate.

In 1847, Poe's wife died of tuberculosis, leaving him

despondent. His own health was precarious, and his financial situation was grim. Still, he hoped to get back on his feet by starting his own magazine or eventually marrying again—but to no avail. In 1849, Poe was found "in great distress" and "in need of immediate assistance" in Baltimore. He was taken by carriage to a hospital, where he died from "congestion of the brain" four days later.

Today, visitors continue to pay their respects to Poe at Baltimore's Westminster Burying Ground, drawn by poems and stories with a timeless truth at their core. As one of his friends noted in 1852, Poe understood "that the mournful, the fearful, even the horrible, allures with irresistible enchantment. He probed this general psychological law, in its subtle windings through the mystic chambers of our being, as it was never probed before, until he stood in the very abyss of its center, the sole master of its effects."

Edgar A Poe

★ ★ ★ ★ ★

GENRES

Horror fiction, crime fiction, detective fiction

BORN	**DIED**
January 19, 1809	October 7, 1849
Boston, Massachusetts	Baltimore, Maryland

Abraham Lincoln

FROM ABRAHAM LINCOLN'S SECOND INAUGURAL ADDRESS, MARCH 4, 1865:

Fondly do we hope, fervently do we pray, that this mighty scourge of war may speedily pass away. Yet, if God wills that it continue until all the wealth piled by the bondsman's two hundred and fifty years of unrequited toil shall be sunk, and until every drop of blood drawn with the lash shall be paid by another drawn with the sword, as was said three thousand years ago, so still it must be said "the judgments of the Lord are true and righteous altogether."

With malice toward none, with charity for all, with firmness in the right as God gives us to see the right, let us strive on to finish the work we are in, to bind up the nation's wounds, to care for him who shall have borne the battle and for his widow and his orphan, to do all which may achieve and cherish a just and lasting peace among ourselves and with all nations.

WHEN ABRAHAM LINCOLN was elected president in November 1860 with less than 40 percent of the popular vote, few could have foreseen that the former one-term congressman from Illinois would achieve lasting fame as one of the nation's greatest leaders. After the South's secession plunged the nation into civil war, Lincoln confronted the crisis with strength of character and remarkable political genius. Assuming the burdens of commander in chief, he called for a massive army of volunteers, he chose and guided military leaders, and he made critical decisions on war tactics and strategies.

Lincoln also shaped the American people's understanding of the meaning of the war and the basic ideals that were at stake. By issuing the Emancipation Proclamation on January 1, 1863, he made the struggle to end slavery an important dimension of the war. With the Gettysburg Address of November 19, 1863, he eloquently called for "a new birth of freedom" and for renewed dedication to the task of ensuring that "government of the people, by the people, for the people, shall not perish from the earth."

After Lincoln appointed Ulysses S. Grant general in chief of the Union Army in March 1864, Grant battled

★ ★ ★ ★ ★

THE 16TH PRESIDENT OF THE UNITED STATES

March 4, 1861 – April 15, 1865

BORN		**DIED**
February 12, 1809		April 15, 1865 (age 56)
Hardin County, Kentucky		Washington, DC

Confederate forces until compelling Robert E. Lee to surrender at Appomattox Court House on April 9, 1865. On the evening of April 14, in the wake of victory celebrations, Lincoln was shot by John Wilkes Booth while attending a play at Ford's Theatre in Washington. He died the following morning.

Despite Lincoln's brief time as a major figure on the national scene, he left an invaluable legacy. Largely because of Lincoln, in the concise words of historian James McPherson, "the republic endured, and slavery perished."

A resident of the White House for six months, artist Francis B. Carpenter painted the above 1864 painting showing the Lincolns with their three sons—although Willie Lincoln, second from left, had died two years earlier.

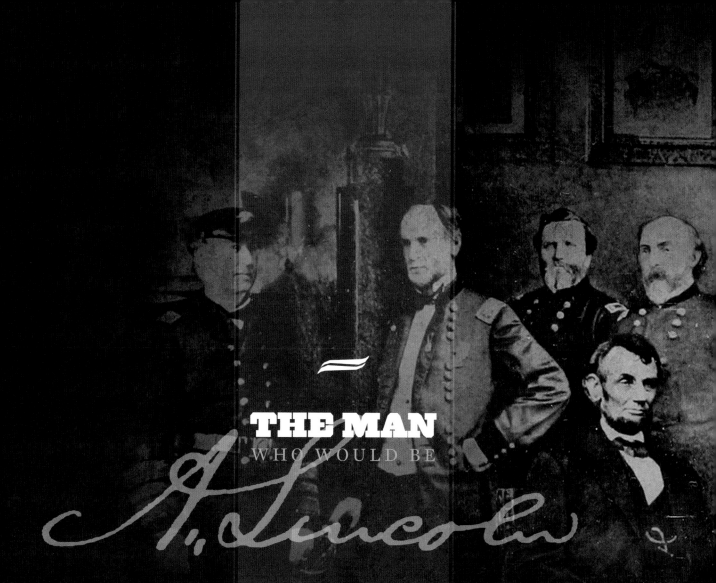

THE MAN
WHO WOULD BE
A. Lincoln

WHEN LINCOLN LEFT his father's household to make his way in the world, he was, by his own later account, a "friendless, uneducated, penniless boy," but his outgoing personality, sense of humor, and storytelling ability won him many friends in the small frontier village of New Salem, Illinois, and hastened his political career. Lincoln served four terms in the state legislature and also practiced law in Springfield, the new state capital, for nearly 25 years.

After serving one term in the U.S. House of Representatives from 1847 to 1849, Lincoln ran for the presidency in 1860. The Republican Party promoted the image of Lincoln as a "rail-splitter," evoking his frontier origins and enhancing his appeal to the workingman. In fact, Lincoln's rise to lawyer and political leader had more to do with his love of learning and his determination to progress beyond his rural roots. Not content with the life of a small farmer, Lincoln worried about how hard it would be "to die and leave one's Country no better than if one had never lived."

LINCOLN · DOUGLAS
DEBATES

LINCOLN WAS LITTLE KNOWN ON the national scene when he ran against Illinois political rival and Democrat Stephen A. Douglas for a Senate seat in 1858. He challenged the incumbent Douglas to a series of debates in which a major point of contention was the institution of slavery and its future in the republic. Held in seven Illinois congressional districts over a period of almost two months, the open-air debates drew unprecedented press coverage and brought Lincoln national recognition.

Although Lincoln failed to wrest the Senate seat from Douglas, he was invited to speak two years later at Cooper Union in Manhattan. In a well-researched speech, he marshaled historical evidence to support his argument that the federal government could legally restrict the spread of slavery. Three months later, he became the Republican presidential nominee.

RAIL-SPLITTER
LAWYER
POLITICIAN
PRESIDENT

ABOUT THE DESIGN TEAM | For these stamps commemorating the 200th anniversary of the birth of Abraham Lincoln, art director Richard Sheaff placed photographs of Lincoln alongside artwork by Mark Summers representing different aspects of Lincoln's life. Summers is known for his scratchboard technique, and his drawings of literary and historical figures regularly appear in the *New York Times* Book Review section.

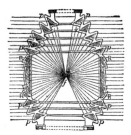

Lighthouses *Gulf Coast*

FOR MORE THAN 150 years, lighthouses have guided ships and other sailing vessels along the Gulf Coast, the picturesque but dangerous thousand-mile stretch between Corpus Christi, Texas, and Key West, Florida. Known as "hurricane alley," the region is inhospitable to lighthouses, and erosion in its swamps and marshlands make it doubly difficult for lighthouses to withstand heavy rains and winds. These five lighthouses are some of the few that remain standing.

Listed on the National Register of Historic Places in 1984, **Matagorda Island Lighthouse** has stood proudly for more than a century near Port O'Connor, Texas. The black tower—which was automated in 1956—is made of cast iron and features a solar-powered light.

Erected on soft, marshy ground in Louisiana, **Sabine Pass Lighthouse** features eight buttresses that stabilize the heavy brick structure and give it a distinct missilelike shape. Completed in 1856, the lighthouse was deactivated in 1952 and is currently closed to the public.

Of all the lighthouses that once stood in Mississippi, **Biloxi Lighthouse** is the only one still standing. Named to the National Register of Historic Places in 1973, the white tower was built in 1848, making it one of the first cast-iron lighthouses in the South.

First lit in 1873, **Sand Island Lighthouse** was an active aid to navigation for 60 years. Once the central attraction on a 400-acre island off the coast of Alabama, this conical tower made of local brick now stands alone, its foundation completely surrounded by water.

Erected in 1876, **Fort Jefferson Lighthouse** (also known as Garden Key Lighthouse) helped warn sea traffic away from the dangerous shoals and reefs that surround the Florida Keys until it was deactivated in 1921. Today the hexagonal lighthouse is part of Dry Tortugas National Park.

MATAGORDA ISLAND, TEXAS

SABINE PASS, LOUISIANA

BILOXI, MISSISSIPPI

SAND ISLAND, ALABAMA

FORT JEFFERSON, FLORIDA

ABOUT THE ARTIST | Although his commissions have included paintings of aviation and space-related subjects for NASA, the U.S. Air Force Academy, and the National Air and Space Museum, veteran stamp artist Howard Koslow is perhaps best known to philatelists for his lighthouses. Including these five, Koslow has painted 25 pictures of lighthouses for U.S. stamps.

Thanksgiving Day
Parade

ON NOVEMBER 30, 1888, a *New York Times* reporter was astonished by the rattle and boom of drums and "the harsh utterances of big and little brass instruments" at Thanksgiving Day parades throughout the city. Costumed revelers filled the streets, while kings and queens and "caricatures of every human oddity" marched and danced in front of raucous crowds. "Down town the noises were probably more abundant than up town," the reporter observed, foreshadowing a new national tradition that was close to catching on: "When they had passed to up-town or Staten Island parks, imitation processions were made up on every block."

Even though it had been only 25 years since President Abraham Lincoln issued a Proclamation of Thanksgiving that recognized the annual holiday, the day of countless parades in 1888 was a sign of things to come. By 1918, newspaper ads touted silk American flags and advised readers to "prepare for Thanksgiving Parade." Soon, large cities and small towns alike were hosting celebrations of their own. From marching bands and colorful floats to large balloons shaped like animals and popular characters, modern Thanksgiving Day parades may dwarf the disorganized revels observed by the 19th-century reporter, but his summation is wonderfully timeless: "Altogether they made up a series of processions that kept the down-town people in a state of wonder and interest for hours."

STAMPS ON PARADE

With visual vignettes that span four stamps, this issuance captures the breadth and excitement of a Thanksgiving Day parade, but the design is also a philatelic curiosity. These stamps are "se-tenant," a term used to describe an attached pair, strip, or block of stamps that differ in design, denomination, or color.

ABOUT THE STAMP ARTIST | To create these stamps, artist Paul Rogers drew on the rich visual history of Thanksgiving Day parades, especially as represented in mid-20th century advertising and poster art. Known for the range of his work, Rogers collaborated with Wynton Marsalis on *Jazz ABZ: An A to Z Collection of Jazz Portraits*, a 2005 book designed to introduce young people to musical greats.

Nature of America

Kelp Forest

SNAILS AND CRABS climb on rocks or creep along the waving blades of kelp. Sea slugs cling to plant life as colorful species of rockfish swim past. A harbor seal eyes a school of anchovies while a blue shark cruises by. At the surface, pelicans, gulls, and cormorants swoop and dive, a symphony of feasting and flying. This is the kelp forest, a remarkable place where life thrives in the shade of giant underwater plants, and where creatures large and small contribute to one of the most intriguing ecosystems on the planet.

Found throughout the world, kelp forests flourish in shallow, cool coastal areas where upwelling brings nutrient-rich waters from the deep sea. A kelp forest has an upper layer called a canopy, but unlike the leafy branches of a land forest, the undersea canopy consists of long fronds at the top of swaying towers of kelp. Lacking roots, kelp instead have holdfasts, rootlike masses that

(continued on page 51)

ABOUT THE ARTIST | John D. Dawson's meticulous eye for detail is evident in his nature paintings for a wide range of articles, posters, guidebooks, postage stamps, and zoo signs. Drawing upon his vast personal files of recorded field observations, debris, and field sketches, Dawson has been the artist behind the Nature of America series since its 1999 debut; each stamp pane is a testimony to his use of specimen studies and consultation with experts.

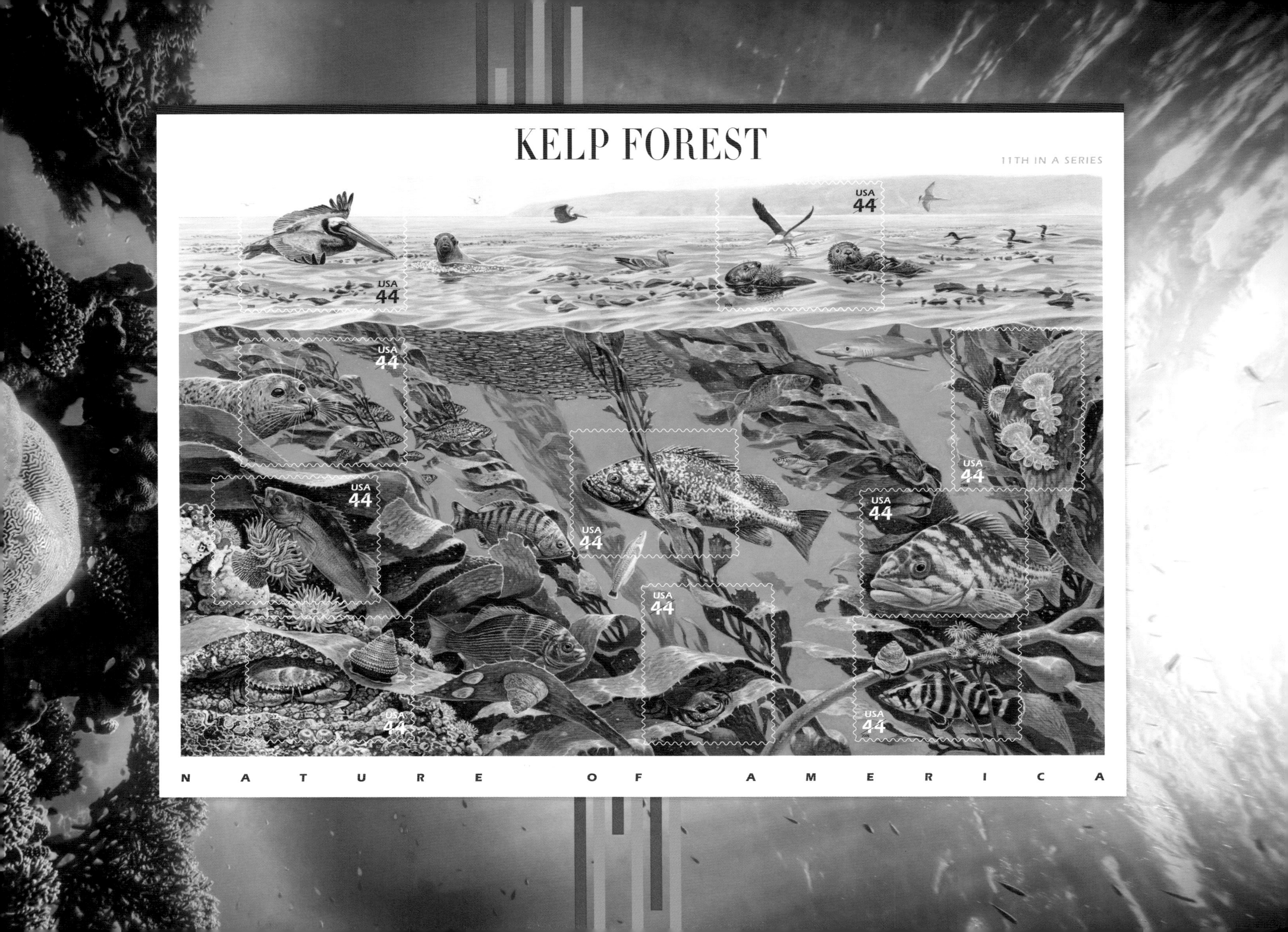
KELP FOREST
11TH IN A SERIES
USA 44
NATURE OF AMERICA

BROWN PELICAN | Remarkably, brown pelicans can spot fish from as high as 60 feet in the air, and the aerial dive that precedes each meal is a wonder to behold. After catching its prey, the pelican drains as much as three gallons of water from its pouch and then swallows the fish whole. Special glands help remove salty fluid from the pelican's system by sending it dripping along grooves on its bill — a fine example of this seabird's adaptation to a highly complex ecosystem.

overgrow and cling to the rocky bottom to hold them in place. The largest species of kelp can grow as much as 2 feet a day, stretching 100 feet or more from the seafloor to the surface and out across the water.

This stamp pane, the eleventh in the Nature of America series, depicts more than 27 species in one kelp forest in the Monterey Bay National Marine Sanctuary, a federally protected area encompassing 5,322 square miles of ocean off the central California coast. Each year, countless visitors observe the upper layers of the kelp forest simply by standing on the coast and marveling at its beauty. With this stamp pane, more Americans may yet become aware of the vital and beguiling realm that lies beneath.

MONTEREY BAY | The stamp pane features a kelp forest off the central California coast. The scene itself is imaginary; a dense grouping of creatures was necessary to illustrate as many species as possible. Even so, all of the species could be encountered at or near the Monterey Bay National Marine Sanctuary, the area featured on the pane. Scientists recommended these species based on their appearance and behaviors in the wild.

The Year of the Ox began on January 26, 2009, and ends on February 13, 2010. Individuals born during this time are said to be hardworking, tolerant, and persistent — but also strong and sometimes a bit stubborn. Famous people born during a Year of the Ox have included George Clooney, Morgan Freeman, President Barack Obama, and Diana, Princess of Wales.

Year of the Ox

CELEBRATING LUNAR NEW YEAR

樂
能
牛

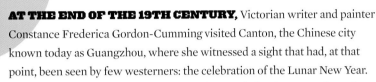

AT THE END OF THE 19TH CENTURY, Victorian writer and painter Constance Frederica Gordon-Cumming visited Canton, the Chinese city known today as Guangzhou, where she witnessed a sight that had, at that point, been seen by few westerners: the celebration of the Lunar New Year.

"[W]e wandered through the strange lantern-lighted streets, where the gorgeous sign-posts are made more attractive by decorations of scarlet cloth and gold flowers," she later wrote. "We wandered about for a couple of hours, in and out of the temples and gardens and strange little shops, buying all manner of odd treasures." Perhaps unsurprisingly, Gordon-Cumming found herself enamored of a particularly appropriate treasure for the holiday: two elegant ceramic lions.

The Celebrating Lunar New Year stamp for 2009 would likewise charm the traveler of yesteryear, featuring as it does a lion's head of the type often worn at Lunar New Year parades. Dancers wear these oversize heads, often made of papier-mâché and bamboo, as they perform for delighted crowds—a spectacle now enjoyed annually in communities across America. The sights and sounds of the Lunar New Year revels tend to overwhelm a first-time viewer, as Gordon-Cumming keenly observed. "The great festival is now fairly ushered in," she wrote, "and certainly there has been noise enough to secure a very lucky year, if noise will do it!"

ABOUT THE STAMP ARTIST | Now a professor of illustration at the Fashion Institute of Technology, Kam Mak was born in Hong Kong and grew up in New York City's Chinatown. His richly colored paintings have adorned the covers of numerous magazines and books, including his first offering as both author and illustrator, *My Chinatown: One Year in Poems.* His artwork for the Year of the Ox stamp was originally created using oil paints on a fiberboard panel.

MAIL USE STAMPS

Literary Arts: RICHARD WRIGHT

ART DIRECTOR AND DESIGNER :: Carl T. Herrman

ARTIST :: Kadir Nelson

The 25th honoree in the Literary Arts series, **Richard Wright (1908–1960)** is best remembered for his controversial 1940 novel, *Native Son*, and his 1945 autobiography, *Black Boy*. Wright drew on a wide range of literary traditions, including protest writing and detective fiction, to craft unflinching portrayals of racism in American society.

POLAR BEAR

ART DIRECTOR AND DESIGNER :: Carl T. Herrman

ARTIST :: Nancy Stahl

This 2009 stamp features a highly stylized illustration of a polar bear (*Ursus maritimus*) by Nancy Stahl, whose designs for the Postal Service include the Florida panther in 2007 and the dragonfly in 2008.

WEDDING RINGS

ART DIRECTOR AND DESIGNER :: Ethel Kessler
PHOTOGRAPHER :: Renée Comet

Intended for use on the RSVP envelope often enclosed with a wedding invitation,
this stamp shows two gold wedding rings resting on a small white pillow and united by a
slender ribbon of white silk.

WEDDING CAKE

ART DIRECTOR AND DESIGNER :: Ethel Kessler
PHOTOGRAPHER :: Renée Comet

Sure to add a touch of beauty and romance to wedding correspondence, this two-ounce
stamp accommodates the heavier weight of an invitation, as well as other mailings such as
oversize cards or small gifts that require extra postage.

U.S. FLAG

ART DIRECTOR AND DESIGNER :: Terrence W. McCaffrey
PHOTOGRAPHER :: Rick Barrentine

Showing a softly folded flag, the photograph featured on this stamp emphasizes
the starry blue field of our national symbol.

THE SIMPSONS

ART DIRECTORS :: Derry Noyes and Claudia Mielnik
DESIGNER AND ARTIST :: Matt Groening

With its 20th year in 2009 as a regularly scheduled half-hour series, *The Simpsons* became
the longest-running comedy in the history of American prime-time television.
The show is a critical and popular favorite and has won multiple Emmys, a Peabody Award,
and numerous other accolades.

Love: KING & QUEEN OF HEARTS

ART DIRECTOR AND DESIGNER :: Derry Noyes

ARTIST :: Jeanne Greco

Paying clever tribute to courtship and romance, this latest issuance in the Love series
includes artwork based on 18th-century French playing cards.

Distinguished Americans: MARY LASKER

ART DIRECTOR AND DESIGNER :: Ethel Kessler

ARTIST :: Mark Summers

Mary Woodard Lasker (1900–1994) was a philanthropist, political strategist, and ardent
advocate of medical research for major diseases. She persuaded the nation's leaders to
adopt dramatic increases in public funding for biomedical research, and her efforts helped
make cancer research a national priority.

DOLPHIN

ART DIRECTOR AND DESIGNER :: Carl T. Herrman   ARTIST :: Nancy Stahl

A marine mammal noted for its high intelligence and playful behavior, the bottlenose dolphin (*Tursiops truncatus*) is found mainly in temperate and tropical waters, where it lives in groups that range in size from two to several hundred.

Scenic American Landscapes:
GRAND TETON NATIONAL PARK, WYOMING

ART DIRECTOR AND DESIGNER :: Ethel Kessler   PHOTOGRAPHER :: Dennis Flaherty

Originally established in 1929, Grand Teton National Park was expanded in 1950 to include much of the adjacent Jackson Hole valley. Now encompassing nearly 310,000 acres, the park is known for the majesty of its rugged mountains that tower some 7,000 feet over glacial lakes and the Snake River Valley.

Scenic American Landscapes:
ZION NATIONAL PARK, UTAH

ART DIRECTOR AND DESIGNER :: Ethel Kessler   PHOTOGRAPHER :: Richard Cummins

Encompassing more than 229 square miles, Zion National Park is characterized by high plateaus and mesas with deep sandstone canyons carved into towering cliffs. Bare expanses of sandstone reveal artifacts and layers of rock that showcase the park's geological history. Approximately 120 miles of hiking trails are available to the 2.5 million people who annually visit the park.

Flags of Our Nation: SET 3

ART DIRECTOR AND DESIGNER :: Howard E. Paine   ARTIST :: Tom Engeman

The Flags of Our Nation series continues with a new set of ten designs. Arranged and issued alphabetically, this third set features nine states—Kentucky through Missouri—plus a tenth Stars and Stripes stamp inspired by the opening lines of "America the Beautiful."

Winter Holidays

ART DIRECTOR AND DESIGNER :: Richard Sheaff
ARTIST :: Joseph Cudd

Intended to evoke gift wraps and Christmas prints, these festive stamps feature popular holiday figures seen on decorations and immortalized in story and song.

Hanukkah

ART DIRECTOR AND DESIGNER :: Carl T. Herrman
PHOTOGRAPHER :: Ira Wexler
MENORAH DESIGNER :: Lisa Regan, Garden Deva Sculpture Company

A photograph of a menorah with nine lit candles appears on the third U.S. stamp to commemorate the joyous festival celebrated by Jews around the world. The Postal Service issued its previous Hanukkah stamps in 1996 and 2004.

KWANZAA

ART DIRECTOR AND DESIGNER :: Carl T. Herrman

ARTIST :: Lloyd McNeill

This stamp features the colors of the Kwanzaa flag: green for growth, red for blood, and black for the African people. The field of green around the borders symbolizes a bountiful harvest, while the family grouping and the hoop held by the girl both symbolize unity.

Christmas: MADONNA AND SLEEPING CHILD BY SASSOFERRATO

ART DIRECTOR AND DESIGNER :: Carl T. Herrman

Currently in the collection of Hearst Castle in California, the painting featured on this stamp is the work of Italian artist Giovanni Battista Salvi (1609–1685), more commonly known as Sassoferrato. The issuance of this stamp coincides with the 400th anniversary of the artist's birth.

CREDITS

COVER AND TITLE PAGE

Stamp art © U.S. Postal Service

TITLE PAGE

PAGE 2 :: (left to right) Jose Fuste Raga/Corbis; Archives Center, National Museum of American History; Behring Center, Smithsonian Institution; The Heads of State; National Archives; CBS Photo Archive/Hulton Archive/Getty Images

INTRODUCTION

PAGE 8 :: (left to right) © Flip Schulke/Corbis and © 1978 George Ballis/Takestock; Rare Book and Manuscript Library, Columbia University; © Chris Low/iStockphoto; Library of Congress, Prints and Photographs Division; Art by Paul Rogers © U.S. Postal Service. Stamp image of J.R. Clifford courtesy of Special Collections Department, W.E.B. DuBois Library, University of Massachusetts Amherst.

PAGE 9 :: AP Photo/Gretchen Ertl

EARLY TV MEMORIES

PAGE 10 :: Photofest

PAGE 11 :: CBS Photo Archive/Hulton Archive/Getty Images

PAGE 12 :: (left) Getty Images; (right) NBCU Photo Bank, image provided by Photofest.

PAGE 13 :: Howdy Doody Photo by: NBC Universal Photo Bank. THE RED SKELTON SHOW © CBS Broadcasting Inc. I LOVE LUCY TM/® & © 2007 CBS Broadcasting Inc. All Rights Reserved. Image of Lucille Ball used with the permission of Desilu, too, LLC. Unforgettable Licensing. Texaco Star Theater Photo by: NBC Universal Photo Bank. You Bet Your Life Photo by: NBC Universal Photo Bank. Groucho Marx™ Groucho Marx Productions, Inc., Los Angeles, CA. Hopalong Cassidy is a registered trademark of U.S. Television Office, Inc. LASSIE TM & © Classic Media, Inc., an Ent. Rights co. Dragnet is a trademark and copyright of Universal Studios. Licensed by Universal Studios Licensing LLLP. All rights reserved. THE PHIL SILVERS SHOW © CBS Broadcasting Inc. KUKLA FRAN & OLLIE is a trademark used under license. © 2009 EML Library Partnership. All rights reserved. "The Ed Sullivan Show"® is a registered trademark of SOFA Entertainment,

Inc. All rights reserved. Image of Ed Sullivan used with the permission of Sullmark Corp. The Dinah Shore Show licensed by the Dinah Shore Living Trust, Beverly Hills, California and Jaffe Partners Limited Partnership, Beverly Hills, California. Alfred Hitchcock and the Hitchcock likeness are trademarks and copyrights of The Hitchcock Trust. PERRY MASON used with permission. THE LONE RANGER TM & © Classic Media, Inc., an Ent. Rights co. THE HONEYMOONERS is a trademark used under license. © 2008 jaglea VIP Corp. All Rights Reserved. Unforgettable Licensing. THE HONEYMOONERS © CBS Broadcasting Inc. THE TWILIGHT ZONE © 2007 CBS Broadcasting Inc. The Tonight Show Photo by: NBC Universal Photo Bank. The rights to the Steve Allen name and likeness is licensed by Meadowlane Enterprises. The rights to Ozzie and Harriet name and likeness is co-owned by David Nelson and the Rick Nelson LLC.

BOB HOPE

Bob Hope® Hope Enterprises, Inc.

PAGE 14 :: Allan Grant/Time & Life Pictures/Getty Images

PAGE 16 :: (top) © Brownie Harris/Corbis

PAGES 16-17 :: (bottom) © Bettmann/Corbis

PAGE 17 :: (top) Courtesy Hope Enterprises, Inc.

LEGENDS OF HOLLYWOOD: GARY COOPER

Gary Cooper licensed by 7 Bar 9 LLC., New York, New York

PAGE 18 :: Photofest

PAGE 19 :: p. 19 (top right) The Pride of the Yankees © 1942 The Samuel Goldwyn, Jr. Family Trust. All Rights Reserved. Courtesy of MGM CLIP+STILL and The Samuel Goldwyn, Jr. Family Trust. Image provided by Photofest; (bottom) Vera Cruz © 1954 Metro-Goldwyn-Mayer Studios Inc. All Rights Reserved. Courtesy of MGM CLIP+STILL. Image provided by Getty Images.

CIVIL RIGHTS PIONEERS

Stamp image of J.R. Clifford courtesy of Special Collections Department, W.E.B. Du Bois Library, University of Massachusetts Amherst

PAGE 20 :: (top) © Bob Adelman/Corbis; (bottom) © Bettmann/Corbis

PAGE 21 :: (background) © Flip Schulke/Corbis; (bottom) © 1978 George Ballis/Takestock

PAGE 22 :: (top) © Flip Schulke/Corbis; (bottom) © Bettmann/Corbis

PAGE 23 :: Library of Congress, Prints and Photographs Division

PAGE 24 :: (left) © Flip Schulke/Corbis; (bottom) Library of Congress, Prints and Photographs Division

PAGE 25 :: (top) © Danny Lyons/Magnum Photos

JUSTICES OF THE SUPREME COURT OF THE UNITED STATES

PAGE 26 :: © Bill Ross/Corbis

PAGE 27 :: (background) National Archives; (top to bottom:) © Bettmann/Corbis; © Corbis; © Bettmann/Corbis; National Archives

BLACK HERITAGE: ANNA JULIA COOPER

PAGE 28 :: Oberlin College Archives

PAGE 29 :: Archives Center, National Museum of American History, Behring Center, Smithsonian Institution

ALASKA STATEHOOD

PAGE 30 :: (top) clipart.com; (bottom) © 2009 Thomas Sbampato/AlaskaStock.com

PAGE 31 :: (clockwise from top left) © Jo Overholt/AlaskaStock.com; © 2009 Anchorage Museum/AlaskaStock.com; © Connie McLain Museum/AlaskaStock.com; © Steven Kazlowski/AlaskaStock.com

OREGON STATEHOOD

PAGE 32 :: (left) ©Noah Strycker/iStockphoto; (bottom) © Edward Martins/iStockphoto

PAGE 33 :: (top) © Jeremy Edwards/iStockphoto; (full page) © Chris Low/iStockphoto

HAWAI'I STATEHOOD

PAGE 34 :: © Jose Fuste Raga/Corbis; (inset) iStockphoto

PAGE 35 :: (top) © Bettmann/Corbis; (bottom right) © Bettmann/Corbis

EDGAR ALLAN POE

PAGE 36 :: (illustration) Emmanuel Polanco, colagene.com

PAGE 37 :: Rare Book and Manuscript Library, Columbia University

PAGE 38 :: Hulton Archive/Getty Images

PAGE 39 :: (illustration) Emmanuel Polanco, colagene.com

ABRAHAM LINCOLN

PAGE 40 :: National Archives

PAGE 41 :: Picture History

PAGES 42-43 :: National Archives

GULF COAST LIGHTHOUSES

PAGE 44 :: Artwork by Howard Koslow © U.S. Postal Service

PAGE 45 :: (map) iStockphoto; (background) Library of Congress, Prints and Photographs Division

PAGES 44-45 :: (background) iStockphoto

THANKSGIVING DAY PARADE

PAGE 46 :: (top) Art by Paul Rogers © U.S. Postal Service; (bottom) © Bettmann/Corbis

PAGE 47 :: Art by Paul Rogers © U.S. Postal Service

NATURE OF AMERICA: KELP FOREST

PAGE 48 :: Norbert Wu/Minden Pictures

PAGE 49 :: © Kristian Sekulic/iStockphoto

PAGE 50 :: © Karen Massier/iStockphoto

PAGE 51 :: (California sea lion and kelp): Flip Nicklin/Minden Pictures; (sea nettle, rockfish, western gull) © Nancy Nehring/iStockphoto; (sea otter) © Jamie Myers/iStockphoto

CELEBRATING LUNAR NEW YEAR: YEAR OF THE OX

PAGE 52 :: Illustration by: The Heads of State

PAGE 53 :: (top left) Matt Pamer/Journey Group; (top right) Calligraphy by Spencer Yu © U.S. Postal Service; (bottom right) artwork by Clarence Lee © U.S. Postal Service

MAIL USE STAMPS

PAGE 56 :: THE SIMPSONS™ & © 2009 Twentieth Century Fox Film Corporation. All rights reserved.

PAGE 61 :: Sassoferrato ©Hearst Castle®/California State Parks

THE 2009 STAMP YEARBOOK

ACKNOWLEDGMENTS

These stamps and this stamp-collecting book were produced by Stamp Services,
Government Relations, United States Postal Service.

JOHN E. POTTER

Postmaster General, Chief Executive Officer

MARIE THERESE DOMINGUEZ

VP, Government Relations and Public Policy

DAVID E. FAILOR

Executive Director, Stamp Services

Special thanks are extended to the following individuals for their contributions to the production of this book:

UNITED STATES POSTAL SERVICE

TERRENCE W. McCAFFREY
Manager, Stamp Development

CINDY L. TACKETT
Manager, Stamp Products and Exhibitions

SONJA D. EDISON
Project Manager

HARPERCOLLINS PUBLISHERS

STEPHANIE MEYERS
Associate Editor

BRUCE NICHOLS
Publisher, Collins Reference

DIANE ARONSON
Senior Copy Chief

SUSAN KOSKO
Production Director

LUCY ALBANESE
Design Director

JOURNEY GROUP, INC.

MICHAEL RYAN
Design Director

ZACHARY BRYANT, KRISTEN KIMMEL
Creative Assistance

GREG BREEDING
Creative Director

JENNIFER ARNOLD
Account Director

PHOTOASSIST, INC.

MARY STEPHANOS, JEFF SYPECK, GREG VARNER
Editorial Consultants

MICHAEL OWENS
Image Coordination

SARAH HANDWERGER, MICHAEL OWENS
Image Rights and Licensing

THE CITIZENS' STAMP ADVISORY COMMITTEE

BENJAMIN F. BAILAR

CARY R. BRICK

DONNA DE VARONA

JEAN PICKER FIRSTENBERG

DR. HENRY LOUIS GATES, JR.

SYLVIA HARRIS

JESSICA HELFAND

I. MICHAEL HEYMAN

JOHN M. HOTCHNER

KARL MALDEN

JOAN A. MONDALE

B. MARTIN PEDERSEN

CLARA RODRIGUEZ